BONES

AN INSIDE LOOK AT THE ANIMAL KINGDOM

First U.S. edition 2020
First published by 20 Watt, an imprint of Bonnier Books U.K., 2018

Library of Congress Catalog Card Number pending
ISBN 978-1-5362-1041-5

19 20 21 22 23 24 TLF 10 9 8 7 6 5 4 3 2 1

Printed in Dongguan, Guangdong, China

This book was typeset in Caviar Dreams and Futura.
The illustrations were created digitally.

BIG PICTURE PRESS
an imprint of
Candlewick Press
99 Dover Street
Somerville, Massachusetts 02144

www.candlewick.com

BONES

AN INSIDE LOOK AT THE ANIMAL KINGDOM

Jules Howard

illustrated by Chervelle Fryer

BPP

CONTENTS

A.

THE WONDER OF BONES

Skeletons are the architecture for much of life on Earth. But your bones have a secret to tell. . . .

Though we humans like to consider ourselves unique, our bones are anything but unique. Look inside the bodies of many animals and you will come to realize that our bones are the same as theirs, just structured differently. This is the hidden beauty of animal skeletons—the same old bones configured hundreds of different ways.

For instance, dogs and cats have nearly all the same bones that we do, even though they walk on four legs. If you look inside their bodies you will see the same four fingers and a thumb, seven neck bones, shoulder blades, a pelvis, a rib cage, and jaws filled with familiar molar teeth, canine teeth, and incisor teeth. The same is true of bears and bats and mice and meerkats—all have the same bones stretched in different ways to assist them in different styles of life. Even fish, a very distant relative of ours, have a skeleton similar to our own—a skull with a jaw that moves up and down at one end, connected to its tail by a long chain of bones (vertebrae) that make up the backbone or spine. Together, creatures with backbones are called vertebrates. If you look inside the bony animals that live on Earth, you will see a simple vertebrate skeleton adapted for a thousand different purposes.

This book is a celebration of bones. On its pages you can see how animals achieve so much with this simple vertebrate body plan. You will see how they leap, how they jump, how they sprint, and how they flap. You will learn how they grasp, how they swim, how they dig, and how they bite and chew.

The story of animals and their success on planet Earth is really a story of skeletons. So turn the pages of this book and learn what makes the bones in us—all of us—so special.

A. There are 206 bones in the human body. Babies are actually born with around 300 bones, but some bones fuse together as skeletons grow.

B. The human skeleton is very much a mammal skeleton. Mammals, such as monkeys, often have two sets of teeth: milk teeth and adult teeth. Most mammals have three tiny ear bones. Most also give birth to live babies, rather than laying eggs with a shell.

C. Birds are all that is left of the dinosaur family. Their skeletons are adapted to a life in the sky. Their wrist bones are fused, and they have a curved breastbone onto which flight muscles attach.

D. Most amphibians lay eggs in water that hatch into tiny fish-like babies (frog and toad babies are called tadpoles). Amphibian skeletons are fish-like and simple, though some species, like frogs, are exceptionally good at adapting to new ways of life.

E. If you lined up every species of bony animal on Earth, most of them (more than 28,000) would be fish. Bony fish (Osteichthyes) have a long spine that can wiggle right and left and a lower jaw that moves up and down.

F. Most reptile skeletons have four legs, though the legs of some lizards and snakes have shrunk over many millions of years so that they are now legless. Most reptiles lay eggs with a protective shell.

WHAT ARE BONES?

Without bones, you and I would be unable to move or know much about the world at all. But bones are about more than body support—bony skeletons help animals in a lot of different ways.

Protection

Many bones provide protection to the body's important organs. The skull of nearly all animals is like a crash helmet that protects the brain. The rib cage protects the heart, stomach, and lungs.

Health

The large bones in our body are filled with bubble-like tissue called marrow. Marrow makes blood. It also makes special white blood cells that fight off infection.

Anchoring

Our bones are linked by special tissues called ligaments. Ligaments keep the bones together and allow them to move without pulling apart the skeleton.

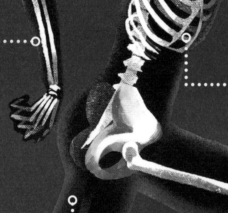

Breathing

In many vertebrates, the rib cage moves in and out to assist with breathing. A membrane covering the lungs is attached to the ribs, and without our ribs we would be unable to breathe.

Movement

Skeletons can be made to move because muscles attach to them. These muscles attach to bones through connector tissues called tendons. When the muscles flex, the tendons pull on the bones and the skeleton moves.

Compact bone, the hard, strong outer layer of bone

Blood vessels supply oxygen and fuel to bone cells.

Bone marrow makes blood cells and stores fat.

BONES vs. CARTILAGE

Sharks and rays have skeletons made of softer and more flexible connective tissue called cartilage. It is lightweight and contains special cells called chondrocytes that produce an elastic-like material, which allows it to spring back into shape. Unlike most bones, cartilage quickly decays after an animal dies. For this reason, studying shark skeletons can be tricky. Usually only their teeth remain, some of which may turn into fossils.

Cartilage is not unique to sharks and rays. A layer of cartilage is also found on the tips of most animal bones, including our own. This cartilage allows bones to move against one another without wearing out. In humans, our noses and ears are also made of cartilage. This is what makes them so bendy.

All vertebrates begin life with a skeleton made of cartilage. In the early months of life, as we grow, the cartilage is gradually replaced by true bone.

WHAT ARE BONES MADE OF?

Bone is eight times stronger than concrete. So what makes it so strong? The outside part of most bones is called compact bone. Here, tiny cylinders of crystallized calcium mixed with special proteins are packed tightly against one another to provide an armor-like coating. This is what gives bones their superstrength. Tiny blood vessels run through the center of each tiny cylinder. This means that inside our bodies, when we're alive, our bones are actually pink!

Spongy bone, the strong, lightweight inner layer of bone

THE FIRST BONES

Haikouichthys is one of the first creatures to have had a hint of skeleton. This simple creature lived 525 million years ago and shared the ocean with many early life-forms. It had a defined skull and a long cord of nerve tissue running down its body. Though it was little more than a swimming worm-like creature, within a few million years this simple body plan would give rise to a new branch of the animal family tree, the vertebrates.

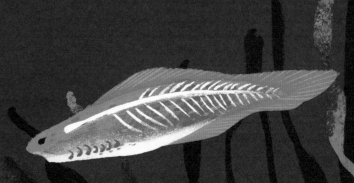

LIFE STORY

Fossils are found in sedimentary rock, which forms in special layers called strata. Often, the deeper scientists dig, the further back in time the fossils they discover date from. By investigating these layers of strata, scientists see how the skeletons of many animals gradually evolve as the years pass.

Generation by generation, over many thousands or millions of years, animal species can gradually change, bit by bit. Fossils are one way for scientists to study how animals have evolved over many millions of years.

THE SCIENCE OF BONES

Sometimes bones can be buried by mud or sand and, over time, are replaced with minerals so that they become fossils. Fossil bones and skeletons are incredibly valuable to scientists, particularly scientists who study ancient life—paleontologists.

Paleontologists carefully dig up and clean fossil bones, many of which are sent to museums where other scientists will study and describe them in special reports. Fossils from dinosaurs, many of

dinosaurs by studying fossils, and new dinosaur species are dug up about once every two weeks.

But bones aren't only for paleontologists. Amateur naturalists, archaeologists, and zoologists also collect and study bones from animals that have recently died. These scientists take measurements of these animal bones and keep them in reference collections that are a bit like libraries. Sometimes, if the bones are still covered in flesh, they use special beetle grubs to clean the remaining meat off

HUMAN REMAINS

Much of what we know about human history is due to the hard work of archaeologists who dig up and study human remains. From bones, these scientists can gather information about the diet and culture of ancient people while also gathering DNA to discover who the bones belonged to and where they were from. By looking at the chemical signature of bones, particularly a natural form of the element carbon (C-14), scientists can also determine how old the bones are.

EVOLUTION

Evolution is perhaps most striking in mammal skeletons. In mammals, a relatively simple mouse-like mammal that lived in the shadow of the dinosaurs appears to have evolved in the most amazing ways into the mammals that we see around us today.

Not all skeletons evolve in obvious ways, however. Some animals hit upon a skeletal structure that proves unbeatable. Turtles, for instance, appeared more than 200 million years ago and have changed very little since that time. Their hard shell, it seems, cannot be bettered, so their skeletal evolution has slowed to a halt.

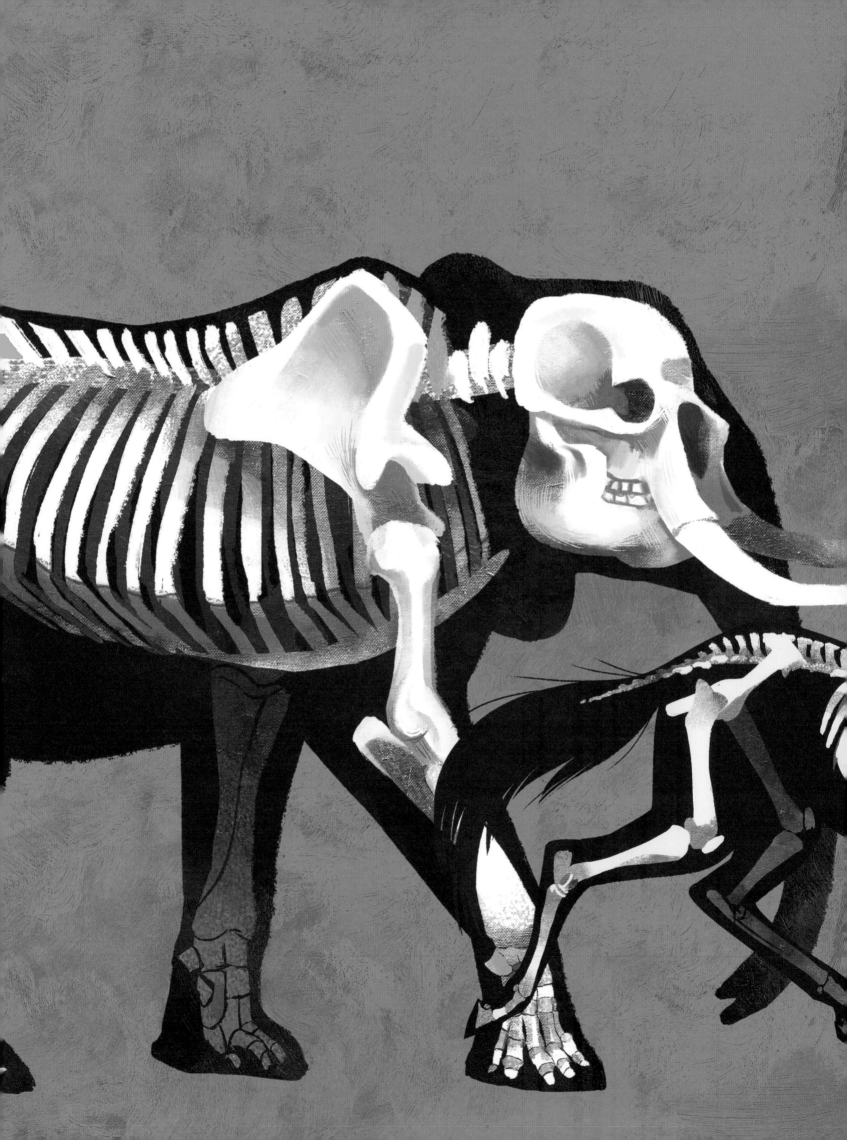

BONES

BITING AND JAWS

Four hundred and thirty million years ago, in the early days of life on Earth, a small family of fish hit upon something truly spectacular. By evolving a long, hinged gill bone along the underside of the mouth, they gained jaws, a muscular mouth capable of pulling apart plants and other animals. This simple bony innovation (called the mandible) allowed these early vertebrates to explore whole new habitats and ways of life. Today, jawed creatures—including humans—rule Earth.

In the modern age, animals use jaws for far more than just eating. Jaws can be used as weapons to fight off rivals. They can be used to suck up ants or snap at passing flies. In snakes, they provide a mechanism for delivering venom. In some dolphins, they can be used to detect electricity. In the case of toothed whales, they can be used as a hearing aid. In fact, in one small family of apes, jaws provide a mechanism through which to utter words and sentences. That family is *Homo sapiens*—human beings.

MEAT EATERS

Many meat-eating mammals have large canine teeth that grip and pull apart prey as well as sharp scissor-like molar and premolar teeth (carnassials) that cut through flesh and, occasionally, bones. In large sharks, including the great white shark, the teeth are triangular, allowing them to slot against one another, creating a scissor-like edge that can cut through flesh.

Some fish-eating vertebrates, such as crocodiles and dolphins, possess long jaws with needle-like teeth, which they use to pin down escaping fish.

Meat-eating mammals have sharp and often large canine teeth.

The carnassials (sha molar and premolar teeth) are used for shearing through fle and bones.

LEAF EATERS

Plant-eating mammals often have large, heavy-duty molar teeth, which they use for crushing leaves and branches. In giraffes, deer, and sheep, the front upper teeth have been replaced by a large muscular pad that can be used to strip leaves off branches.

SEED EATERS

Rodents are specialized gnawers. Their long incisors can chisel through nuts and other hard foods. These incisors are unusual because they continue growing throughout life. Rodents keep them sharp by rubbing them against one another.

Most rodents can have up to twenty-two teeth with a large gap called a diastema between them.

TOOTH REPLACEMENT

Having loose teeth during childhood is unique to mammals. Nearly all mammals have two sets of teeth in their life—the baby (milk) teeth and adult teeth. In most cases, if mammals lose an adult tooth, it won't be replaced.

Reptiles are better able to replace lost teeth. An adult crocodile, for instance, may go through fifty sets of teeth in its lifetime, regrowing 3,000 teeth in total. The same is likely to have been true for their dinosaur cousins.

Sharks are famous for their ability to replace teeth. Like a conveyor belt, rows of razor-sharp teeth grow from the jaw and are slowly flipped around to the front of the mouth. An adult shark may go through 30,000 teeth in its life.

SPERM WHALE
Physeter macrocephalus

Right now, as you read these words, somewhere on Earth a sperm whale is fighting with a giant squid deep underwater. Due to a number of impressive adaptations, it is likely that the sperm whale will emerge as the victor.

The sperm whale finds squid using the largest brain in the animal kingdom, which sits within a truly impressive skull. Their brain is five times heavier than a human brain. A set of complex organs attaches to the roof of the enormous skull through which powerful and focused clicking sounds are made. The echoes from these clicks are received and channeled toward the brain through the whale's lower jaw. Like dolphins, the sperm whale hunts through echolocation.

The jaw of the sperm whale has eighteen to twenty-six teeth that resemble those of a *Tyrannosaurus rex* in size and strength. Their long jaws can be used to hold squid in place before swallowing, though mature male sperm whales sometimes use them against one another when competing for the attentions of a female.

Diving to extreme depths to hunt prey is not easy. First, sperm whales need power. They possess the largest tail for their size of any whale, which drives them deep into the water. Sperm whale skeletons have adapted to cope with the immense pressure of the deep sea by evolving ribs bound to the spine by a special flexible cartilage.

This hinge-like structure allows the rib cage to collapse as the whale dives without shattering any bones.

Even with these adaptations, they pay a price for their deep dives—adult sperm whale bones often show the telltale pits and tiny cracks that signal bouts of decompression sickness. Still, theirs is a prey worth stalking—no other mammal has made a meal of giant squid quite like the sperm whale.

The sperm whale's lopsided skull allows it to locate prey from many different directions.

The flexible rib cage allows the lungs to collapse to accommodate the pressure from deep dives.

The whale still has five finger-like bones in its pectoral fins—a relic of its past.

Each tooth is cone-shaped, and weighs about 2 pounds/1 kilogram.

TIGER
Panthera tigris

As far as killers go, few skeletons can match that of a tiger. Every single curve or ridge on its bones hints at its predatory lifestyle. And nowhere is this more apparent than its skull. Tigers have shorter, stouter faces than many predators. Unlike crocodiles, which must snap at passing prey with long jaws, tigers pull down their prey with killer claws. Their jaws aren't for catching. They are for killing.

Tiger canines are among the longest of all big cats, sometimes measuring up to 3 inches/8 centimeters long. Tigers use them to bite down on the neck bones of their prey, often severing the spinal cord of a potential meal within seconds with a single bite. As in all big cats, these canines are lined with pressure-sensitive nerves that allow tigers to use their teeth to feel the location for the perfect bite.

The impressive jaw muscles that tigers use to administer their killer blows pass through large holes called zygomatic arches on the sides of the skull. A distinctive arch that runs along the sagittal crest at the top of the skull increases the area to which these muscles can attach.

Tigers have thirty teeth, which is fewer than most predators. They have sacrificed tooth number for tooth strength.

A tiger's foreleg has a very strong bone that supports a huge amount of muscle tissue. This helps it grab hold of struggling prey.

Compared to those of other mammals, the back teeth of a tiger are especially sharp. When it opens and closes its jaws, the molars and premolars of the upper and lower jaw slot together perfectly like blades on a pair of scissors. The tiger's tough jaws exert enormous pressure across these molars, meaning that these teeth are strong enough to shear through tough flesh and even bone. A tiger's bite can generate seven times the pressure that a human bite can.

Even the front teeth, called incisors, have a function. Tiger incisors can be used to strip meat from bone or, occasionally, to pluck feathers from birds. These, along with the giant front-facing eye sockets, called orbits, that contain enormous eyes for spotting prey, and the enlarged skull that houses an impressive brain, give tigers a suite of killer adaptations few predators can match. The tiger possesses an almost weaponized skull, perfected for catching and killing prey.

Tigers have long bones in their hind legs that allow them to spring onto unsuspecting prey.

While humans have thirty-three vertebrae, snakes can have up to 500 vertebrae, depending on the species.

Unlike boas and pythons, rattlesnakes have no remains of a pelvis or any limbs in skeletons. Parts of the body that are useless, like a pelvis on a snake, are called vestigial structures.

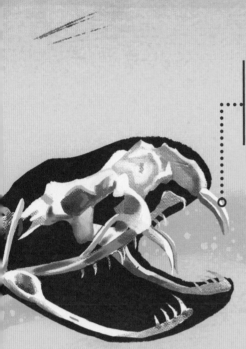

The eastern diamondback has the longest fangs for its size of any rattlesnake.

EASTERN DIAMONDBACK RATTLESNAKE
Crotalus adamanteus

Occasionally reaching lengths of 6½ feet/2 meters or more, the eastern diamondback rattlesnake is the heaviest venomous snake in the world. It lies hidden and waits for passing rats and rabbits to accidentally move too close before striking its venomous fangs toward them at lightning speed.

The rattlesnake's fangs are hollow and inject the prey with poison, which begins to act as the prey runs away. Once bitten, the prey rarely lasts long. The diamondback rattlesnake follows a scent trail toward the prey's incapacitated body and then swallows it whole.

Where most vertebrates have only one part of the skull that moves—the jaw—many of the bones that make up a snake's skull can shift and move against one another; they are held together loosely by elastic ligaments that can pull bones back into place after being stretched. Famously, this means that snakes can swallow prey many times the size of their head.

To pull large prey successfully down their throat, snakes can move the left and right sides of their jaws independently. Using this adaptation, they can slowly alternate their jaws over their meal, stretching their mouth around the prey's body until it is fully enclosed and ready to be swallowed. Their ribs are loose and can easily spread apart once prey makes it to the stomach. Theirs is a skeleton that stretches like no other.

Eastern diamondback rattlesnakes like to shelter in gopher burrows. When threatened by predators, they can rear up like a coiled spring onto the lower half of their body and, using powerful muscles attached to their ribs and spine, strike with their fangs in self-defense. As the name implies, they can also rattle their tail.

The rattlesnake's famous rattle is actually made of segments of shed skin rather than bone. The muscles that work this rattle are the fastest known, capable of firing at fifty times per second or more.

DIGGING

Moving through soil takes time and requires an incredible amount of effort. Yet, for the animals that master it, this subterranean way of life offers rich rewards by way of untapped food resources and shelter from predators or extreme weather.

The skeletons of most digging animals require something spade-like to move soil. In moles and other smaller subterranean mammals, it is the paws that provide the digging surface. In armadillos and anteaters, it is the claws. Many toads use their hind legs as spades. By churning up the soil around them, they can shuffle backward into the soil, leaving only their eyes exposed. The African bullfrog can use its long back legs to dig channels that provide water for its developing tadpoles. But other animals use a host of other anatomical features to help them dig.

THE BIGGEST DIGGER

For a long time, a series of enormous burrows in Brazil mystified scientists. Up to 6½ feet/2 meters deep and 13 feet/4 meters in width, the cavernous tunnels were thought to be archaeological remains of some kind. The truth turned out to be far stranger. Scratch marks were found on the walls of the caves: the tunnels had been dug by the claws of an unknown giant mammal.

We now know that these tunnels were dug by the extinct giant ground sloth, a cousin of armadillos and anteaters. At 4.4 tons/ 4 metric tons and measuring up to 20 feet/6 meters from head to tail, this giant herbivore possessed sickle-shaped claws useful for digging and pulling down tall branches upon which it would feed.

HEADBUTTING

Caecilians are worm-like amphibians that dig through wet soil. After anchoring their tail into position, they thrust their head through the earth like a battering ram. Their skulls are pointed, and fused in various places to provide extra strength.

SAND SWIMMING

Golden moles home in on the telltale movements of insects by feeling for their vibrations in the sand and then "swimming" toward them. Though not closely related to true moles, golden moles possess the same fusiform (bullet-shaped) skeleton and the same powerful forearms. Their foreclaws resemble tiny pickaxes.

DRILLING FOR DINNER

Woodpeckers are famous for their long, pointed beaks, which they use to drum on and drill into tree trunks in search of insects. Woodpeckers' skulls have plate-like bones with a special spongy structure that helps distribute the impact of each hammer-like blow.

TEETH TUNNELING

The naked mole rat uses its long incisor teeth to tunnel. Naked mole rats are rather like ants and wasps. Sterile workers are in charge of digging tunnels to find roots and tubers. Together, they chew a tunnel system that can stretch up to 3.1 miles/5 kilometers in length.

EUROPEAN MOLE
Talpa europaea

The most celebrated mole bone is the extended sesamoid bone in their wrist. It has become almost claw-like. In life, this strange appendage is covered with skin. Unlike true fingers, it has no joints. This unusual adaptation extends the surface area of the paw while adding strength and extra firmness to the digging blades. Mole paws work like giant shovels.

Moles are one of a few mammals that have sesamoid bones adapted in such a way. Others include pandas (for grasping) and elephants (for bearing weight). Sesamoids are the go-to bones for acquiring new fingers.

Moles are highly adapted to detect and then kill prey, mostly invertebrates like beetles and earthworms. Unlike those of other small mammals, mole skulls have a large empty space at the front in which are found unusual arrangements of curly bones called turbinates that improve the mole's sense of smell. Their teeth are sharp, especially the large upper canines used to bite and paralyze their prey, which they carry to special underground storage. Moles can eat around half of their body weight each day.

Though you may never have considered them so, moles are extremely well-muscled. They possess enlarged lever-shaped ulna bones in their forearms that allow more space for the giant muscles required to push through their subterranean habitat.

The eye holes (orbits) are dramatically reduced—eyes serve no purpose in a world without light.

The five front claws are permanently turned outward.

In fact, most of the bones in their forearms are covered with special ridges, called processes, onto which muscles and tendons attach. A special extension bone called the keel increases the surface area to which the pectoral muscles in the chest attach. Some moles can dig tunnels 656 feet/200 meters long, which is equivalent to a human digging through 1½ miles/2.5 kilometers of soil with his or her bare hands.

With their well-muscled, top-heavy skeleton, moles are built like an Olympic swimmer. Yet the substance they swim through isn't water. It's soil.

The armor is formed in twenty-four sections that can overlap, allowing the pink fairy armadillo to roll into a ball.

PINK FAIRY ARMADILLO

Chlamyphorus truncatus

The pink fairy armadillo is the world's smallest and most elusive armadillo. With its torpedo-shaped skeleton, it burrows beneath Argentina's desert-like shrublands, searching for ants and insect larvae.

On both its front and hind legs are enormous claws that slice through the soil and sand. Its eyes and ears are small and very mole-like. To prevent its tunnels from collapsing, it uses its wide tail to firm up the soil as it digs.

Armadillos are well known for their hard bony covering. This protective armor consists of two layers: an upper surface rich in keratin, which is the same protein found in mammal horn, hair, and nails; and a harder, bony surface deeper beneath the skin made up of interlocking sheets of solid bone called osteoderms. Armadillos are the only living mammal group to have hit upon the evolution of this kind of armor. In fact, beneath the skin, armadillos resemble turtles.

In the pink fairy armadillo this armor is dramatically reduced. Adapted to desert environments, fairy armadillos have special blood vessels near the surface of the plates that release excess heat and keep the body cool. These blood vessels are what give the pink fairy armadillo its unusual color. Essentially, when it gets hot, it blushes.

Armadillos have molars like those of a rabbit.

The claws of the pink fairy armadillo are so long that it can have trouble walking on flat surfaces.

Though they are less armored than other armadillos, their shell still offers plenty of protection from most predators. Indeed, like many armadillos, the pink fairy armadillo can roll up into a protective ball.

Armadillos, anteaters, and tree sloths are a distinct and unusual part of the mammal family tree. They are called xenarthrans, which means "strange joints," because their vertebrae link together in a way that strengthens the lower back and hips, allowing for a more powerful digging stance.

GREATER BILBY
Macrotis lagotis

The greater bilby is known as a "scratch digger." Each of its forearms works like the bucket of a mechanical digger, clawing sand downward toward the hind legs, which kick the sand backward. When furiously pumping these bucket-like paws, it shifts an impressive amount of sand. Within minutes, the greater bilby can barely be seen at all.

Bilby shelters are spiral-shaped burrows up to 10 feet/3 meters long and 6½ feet/2 meters deep. When hungry predators attempt to dig them out, bilbies have been known to frantically extend the tunnel in the other direction to get out of harm's way.

The greater bilby has shorter bones in the forearms than many marsupials, which allow its arms to scratch up and down faster. It also possesses three stout claws on its forearms, along with two unclawed toes that help sweep sand downward.

Unlike moles and fairy armadillos, the greater bilby does not spend all its time underground. Instead, it moves from burrow to burrow, sometimes occupying home ranges that span 3 miles/5 kilometers. Although they possess kangaroo-like bones in the hind legs, they trot upon all four legs while moving, rocking backward and forward in a manner that is almost like that of a rocking horse.

Living in the arid regions of central Australia means that the greater bilby has to find a variety of food sources to survive. Greater bilby teeth are able to pull apart a range of items, including grubs, fungi, seeds, and fruit. Their long, pointed skull is adapted for pushing in the sand, a behavior that helps them smell for potential food buried nearby.

Like all marsupials, the greater bilby has a pouch. As with wombats and marsupial moles, their pouch points backward so that it doesn't fill with sand while they dig.

The well-developed ears suggest that the greater bilby has excellent hearing. Their ears are hairless, which may help regulate body temperature.

The well-developed digging forearms weigh down the upper body, meaning that the bilby moves on four legs rather than two.

The greater bilby has a tail that ends in a spur, or nail-like structure. Nobody is sure yet what function this strange tail performs.

Unlike monkeys and apes, sloths have adapted to life without evolving fingers. Instead, they use large, sickle-like claws to latch onto the branches of trees.

Human hand

GRASPING AND CLAWS

By turning the pages of this book, you are doing something most animals cannot. A complicated network of twenty-seven bones in your hand and fingers is allowing you to grasp and carefully manipulate sheets of paper. Only humans, monkeys, and apes (together called primates) can achieve manual dexterity like this.

Unlike most bones, the bones in our fingers have no muscles attached. They are pulled by special tendons that attach to muscles in the palm and wrist. You can see these tendons moving when you look at the inside of your wrist while wiggling your fingers.

Primates evolved grasping hands as an adaptation to life in the trees. Over time, their claws gave way to flatter fingernails and large fleshy fingertip pads that assist with grip. But grasping is not unique to primates. Many other creatures have bony adaptations that assist with carefully gripping a host of objects.

Try using your thumb to touch each of your fingers. Animals that can manage this feat are said to have true opposable thumbs. Opposable thumbs help them to manipulate objects and allow some species to use tools.

Koalas have two opposable thumbs on each paw that assist them with gripping branches. Their second and third toes have also fused, creating a muscular "superfinger" with two claws.

Using their opposable thumbs, chimpanzees can carefully select and prepare special sticks that they use to fish for termites or ants and even to scoop the marrow out of the bones of monkeys, like a sort of primitive spoon. They have also been spotted using sharpened sticks for hunting.

PREHENSILE TAILS

Some animals have long, muscular tails that help them to grasp objects or that allow them to hang from nearby vegetation. These are prehensile tails. Seahorses use their prehensile tails to anchor themselves to seaweed so that they aren't washed away by strong currents. The so-called climbing salamanders use their muscular tails as a prop to help them move up trees. Chameleons use their more mobile prehensile tails to assist with movement between branches while in the treetops.

BABY ON BOARD

Some animals use their jaws as a grasping device to carefully pick up babies. Crocodiles carefully scoop up their young in their mouths, keeping them safe from snakes and other predators.

Large zygomatic arches, combined with a jutting jaw (prognathism) and enormous canine teeth, make chimpanzee bites very powerful.

As in all apes (including humans), the tail is dramatically reduced and has shortened into a fused bone called the coccyx.

The long, curved fingers and opposable thumbs are perfect for getting around and using tools. Chimpanzees have been known to use sticks to get food, stones to open nuts and fruit, and crushed leaves to soak up water.

CHIMPANZEE
Pan troglodytes

It is almost impossible to look at a chimpanzee skeleton without noticing the similarities to our own. This is because, like them, we have inherited an ape skeleton from an unknown ancestor that we shared seven million years ago.

Look closely, however, and you will notice the differences. Where human bones are adapted for marathon-runner-like endurance, chimpanzee skeletons remain more multipurpose, adapted for a forest habitat with many unique ways of finding food and water.

First, the arms and hands. The bones within the hands allow chimpanzees to manipulate objects, but crucially, they can also be used as extra supports to assist movement. The bones in the hands and feet, called phalanges, are curved compared to our own, which is an adaptation seen in apes that climb and walk on their knuckles. Yet their arms are also vital for supporting body weight. This quadruped lifestyle means that chimpanzee skeletons differ in their posture compared to those of humans. Chimpanzees' legs are set wide apart, and they transfer their weight from side to side when they walk. Their pelvis is long and thin, providing a rigid structure that keeps them upright with minimal effort, assisted by long bones within the forearms that support weight. Most noticeably, the hole through which the spinal cord plugs into the skull, called the foramen magnum, is at the back of the skull in chimpanzees and other apes—their torso fits behind the skull rather than below it, like our own.

Like all apes, chimpanzees have opposable thumbs that are capable of moving freely and independently. Yet they possess something we do not. Chimpanzees have a toe-thumb on each foot. This elongated toe-thumb is vital for gripping branches and trunks while climbing.

GIANT PANDA
Ailuropoda melanoleuca

It is mind-boggling to think that the Western world only came to know about the panda relatively recently. For millennia, this elusive bear hid in China's bamboo forests, unseen even by the human residents with whom it shared its habitat. Then it all changed. In the twentieth century, the panda received global attention, and its host of unique skeletal adaptations became known to scientists for the first time.

Pandas are almost unique among mammals because they possess an extra finger. Rather than the standard mammal paw-plan—four fingers and a thumb—pandas possess five fingers and an opposable pseudo-thumb, which they use to grip bamboo while chewing. Though it does have a tough pad like the other fingers, this extra digit is unusual in that it has no claw and it cannot bend. It is not a true finger, but rather an extension of a sesamoid bone in the wrist.

The only other bear-like animal to have evolved a similar sixth pseudo-finger is also a bamboo eater—the red panda (actually not a panda, but a weasel-like creature). Natural selection does this sometimes, favoring the same trait in distantly related creatures to get the same job done. This is called convergent evolution.

The panda's skull shape is that of a once-carnivorous bear that is evolving to become ever-more vegetarian. The wide molars have been co-opted for chewing plants rather than biting through bones. The zygomatic arches are wider, too, allowing for larger and more effective jaw muscles that provide the power to crunch, munch, and swallow.

Pandas also possess a relatively long tail for a bear. Though only 4–6 inches/10–15 centimeters long, this white tail has its uses. Most notably, it can be used like a paintbrush to smear special odors that come from the panda's rear end onto rocks and trees. These stinky secretions help wild pandas keep in touch with one another. Theirs is the second longest of all bear tails, outsized only by that of the sloth bear.

Compared to other bears, pandas have fewer vertebrae. This may be an adaptation that helps pandas spend more time sitting upright.

Pandas have a bigger skull for their size than most bears. Their skulls are filled with muscles that help them chew bamboo.

The skull and teeth have adapted to chewing plants over time, and their molars now resemble those of horses or elephants. They are seven times larger than those of a human.

On their hind legs, pandas have sharp claws that help them to climb trees.

RED HOWLER MONKEY
Alouatta seniculus

For howler monkeys, a life in the trees comes courtesy of a tail almost unmatched in nature. Wrapped around a branch, the howler monkey's long tail can easily support its entire body weight. Creatures that can manage such a feat have prehensile tails.

The tail of the red howler monkey contain numerous vertebrae. Though small, each tiny vertebra allows for many large muscle attachments. This means that howler monkey tails are quite flexible and far stronger than they look. Almost like the tentacle of an octopus, the red howler monkey's tail can grip, pull, and carefully grasp and manipulate items of food. The red howler monkey uses its tail to balance while climbing.

As well as a grasping tail, howlers have hands and feet that have wide separations between the second and third digits and provide extra grasping options.

Red howler monkeys have a larger jawbone than other howler monkeys, which assists them in their leaf-based diet. Their jaws contain strong, shearing molar teeth used for chewing and slicing plant matter. Beneath this jawbone is an unusual bony structure called the hyoid bone. This bone works like an echo chamber, allowing howler monkeys to make arguably the loudest noise of any land animal, which is audible almost 3 miles/5 kilometers away. Howler monkeys use these calls to mark their territory and encourage rivals to move on.

Howler monkeys are unique among South American monkeys in having a hairless patch on their tail (the "friction pad"), which helps with gripping. Incredibly, this special patch has markings unique to each monkey—like a fingerprint.

A red howler monkey's tail is 23–36 inches/60–80 centimeters long and is very strong. It can support the monkey's entire weight.

Howler monkeys' calls can be heard from up to 3 miles/5 kilometers away. They are able to make such loud noises due to the hyoid bone in their throat. They also have a very large mandible (jawbone).

Red howler monkeys have no specialized thumbs. They grasp most objects using the second and third digits of their hands.

HOLDING WEIGHT

Though many science-fiction stories like to imagine 300-foot/90-meter creatures like Godzilla or King Kong, the truth is that bony animals on Earth could never evolve to be so large and walk upon two legs. If they were, their leg bones and joints would fracture like tiny twigs.

This is because animal skeletons are pulled downward by an unseen force, gravity. The scaling effects of gravity mean that increasing the size of an object by ten times would make it one thousand times heavier. This causes problems for giant animals. The larger an animal becomes, the more it must invest in bones to keep it from collapsing.

Large vertebrates solve the problems of gravity through a variety of skeletal adaptations that help to keep them from falling apart under their own weight.

HOW DID THE DINOSAURS DO IT?

The long-necked sauropod dinosaurs reached a size far greater than we see in modern-day animals. Some species, such as *Argentinosaurus huinculensis*, were longer than three buses and may have weighed as much as ten elephants. The secret to their size was a complex system of air-filled cavities in their long bones that kept their skeletons light and strong. Sauropods also had giant cylinder-shaped legs, with bones that dwarf those of modern-day animals. The femur, or thigh bone, of *Argentinosaurus*, for instance, was significantly longer and heavier than that of an adult human.

Argentinosaurus femur 7 feet/2.25 meters

TAKE A WEIGHT OFF

There is one environment on Earth that allows some animals to grow to a larger size—the oceans. Denser than air, water provides a cushion against the effects of gravity. It is no surprise that the largest mammals on Earth exist in the oceans. Some, like the manatee, can no longer return to land—its skeleton could not support the weight of its body.

PILLARS OF STRENGTH

The legs of large land animals are often cylindrical, spreading the weight of each leg over a wide surface area. In elephants, the round feet are lined with special protective tissues that add cushioning, rather like comfortable shoes.

The largest bone in many land-living vertebrates is the femur bone in the thigh. This cylinder-shaped bone bears much of the weight of the skeleton and is loaded with compact bone. In humans, the femur can handle about 6.6 tons/6 metric tons of pressure—roughly equivalent to the weight of four cars.

Elephant femur 3 feet/90 centimeters

Human femur 1½ feet/48 centimeters

The bones in the ball-and-socket joint would not withstand incredible friction without these cartilaginous zones.

WEAR AND TEAR

In larger animals, cartilaginous zones between each bone become ever more important. This squishy tissue acts like the oil in a hinge, reducing friction as bones move against one another. Even with this useful adaptation, however, bones can only withstand the forces of gravity for so long before a range of ailments occur. In humans, bone ailments most often show themselves as backaches or joint pain in the legs and hips.

WILD HORSE
Equus ferus

Horse skeletons appear to achieve the impossible. They allow a large, heavy-bodied grass eater to sprint for longer and faster than any predator. They achieve this feat through a host of adaptations, many of which are as much about reducing wear and tear as they are about adding strength and power.

In the limb bones of horses, one can see clearly the fusing of crucial weight-supporting bones like the radius and ulna in the forelimbs and the tibia and fibula in the hind limbs. This fusing of bones limits the rotational movement of the limbs while running, allowing the stability required to support such a heavy-bodied creature while sprinting. Other adaptations allow for greater speed. The long, thin shoulder blades enable a lengthy stride. This, along with the long limbs, allows the horse to cover more distance with each forward thrust.

Most celebrated of all horse skeletal adaptations are the hooves. These act like shock absorbers while the horse is running, distributing energy evenly back into the limbs.

Horses have large eye sockets that sit high up on their skull, giving them an almost 360-degree vision of potential predators while their heads are in the grass.

Horses' teeth continue to erupt through the gums as the grinding surface of the teeth is worn down by chewing over the years.

Although hooves look like unique skeletal additions, each hoof represents a single mammalian finger that has adapted to hold weight over millions of years. Their ancestors' fossils suggest that the other fingers shrank to help minimize the number of joints in the foot, reducing the number of components that can suffer wear-and-tear damage over time. In effect, today's hooves act like running blades and are incredibly efficient at absorbing and redistributing energy, with very few parts that can go wrong.

Many modern humans still depend on horses for travel, for sport, for work, and for farming. They have strength and athleticism almost unrivalled in nature.

Horses evolved over millions of years in grasslands rich in predators, where only the fastest and most athletic individuals endured.

The different ways that animals move are called gaits. A horse can walk, trot, canter, and gallop. The gallop is the fastest gait, averaging 25–30 miles/40–48 kilometers per hour.

The tusks protrude from the upper jaw and are in fact giant mammalian incisors.

AFRICAN BUSH ELEPHANT
Loxodonta africana

At almost 13 feet/4 meters tall and sometimes weighing more than 11 tons/10 metric tons, the African bush elephant is the largest, heaviest land animal on Earth today. This is an animal built to withstand gravity.

Most notable about their skeletons are the four pillar-like legs. They hang like columns beneath the body, providing direct support underneath the barrel-like rib cage. The leg bones of the African bush elephant are long and thick, with lightweight, ultra-strengthening filling that makes them almost spongy in places.

Unlike in many herbivorous mammals, the elephant pelvis points downward, just like in the human skeleton. Likewise, the forelimbs are held firmly in place by a pair of sturdy shoulder blades, called the scapulae. The radius and ulna bones in the forelimbs are twisted and have fused, which provides extra strength.

The African bush elephant spreads its weight upon five true toes that remain hidden within a layer of tissue in life, covered with tough skin. Like the panda, it has an enlarged sesamoid bone that works a little like a sixth finger, offering added support on each foot.

Elephants do not have a collarbone, but their large shoulder blades give them the support they need.

The elephant's tail is very bony, containing up to 31 vertebrae. It is used mainly to swat away flies.

The radius and ulna have twisted and fused, giving them extra strength and support.

The bottom of the elephant's foot is mainly composed of a special fatty tissue, which offers elastic properties that help turn each foot into a gigantic shock absorber when the elephant walks or runs. This is why elephant footsteps are so famously quiet.

The African bush elephant has an extremely large skull held up by the vertebrae in its neck, which are short and nearly horizontal to the ground. These special neck vertebrae have added spiny hooks onto which muscles attach, providing the power needed to lift the skull and its two enormous tusks.

These tusks, prized by poachers, are little more than highly modified incisor teeth. They replace the milk teeth in the elephant's first year of life and grow continuously at a rate of around 6$\frac{1}{2}$ inches/17 centimeters a year.

Like the largest dinosaurs, elephants have had to dedicate much of their skeleton to the demands of holding up their vast bulk. In fact, the African bush elephant skeleton accounts for 16 percent of its total body weight, notably more than most mammals of such a large size.

COMMON HIPPOPOTAMUS
Hippopotamus amphibius

The common hippopotamus has a skeleton built to sink. Their barrel-shaped rib cage, heavy-boned legs, and enormous skull provide the weight necessary to bounce along river- and lakebeds, which they do with a peculiar kind of grace when under the water.

The common hippopotamus hangs its 1.65-ton/1.5-metric-ton weight upon a thick spinal column, made of extra-strong vertebrae that fit together like a rigid iron beam. Their thirteen stout ribs are bent into a barrel-like cage and help contain the hippo's enormous gut.

As with elephants, the scapulae point downward, attaching to vertical pillar-like legs that provide extra support.

The common hippopotamus is a fantastic example of a graviportal skeleton—a skeleton evolved to bear great weight. Yet hippos carry their weight on land, too, running in short bursts of up to 18 miles/30 kilometers per hour while scaring off intruders. This violent territoriality is what makes hippos one of the deadliest animals on Earth.

Some areas of the common hippo's limb bones are osteosclerotic: especially strengthened with compact bone.

Hippopotamuses have long jaws with a hinge that is very far back in the skull. This allows them to open their jaws almost 180 degrees. The orbits that hold their eyes are raised onto the top of the skull, allowing the hippo to scan for rivals while still in the water.

Their teeth are very large. The lower incisors of the common hippopotamus can measure more than 15½ inches/40 centimeters and, as in rodents, they continue growing throughout life and can be sharpened by grinding them together. They mostly eat grass, though they will sometimes eat decaying dead animals, called carrion, when food is scarce.

These teeth are used mostly in combat, displayed as a warning or used as weapons during attack. They can also be used to attack predators. A large muscle-laden sagittal crest on the skull means that hippos can bite with twice the force of a lion, easily enough to scare off even large crocodiles and ensure that snap-happy tourists stay far back.

A hippo's bite force can exceed 8,100 newtons.

Each of the hippo's four well-developed toes ends in a distinctive nail.

FITNESS FLAGS

Many grass eaters like springbok indulge in a strange behavior called pronking. They can leap $6\frac{1}{2}$ feet/2 meters vertically into the air, lifting all four feet off the ground in a stiff stance while bending their heads low. The behavior may help indicate to predators that they are fit and healthy and not worth chasing.

JUMPING

For bony creatures, becoming airborne even for a few moments requires a lot of energy. Yet many animals need to hop or jump to stay alive. Some animals, including jerboas and wallabies, jump to travel from place to place. Some animals, like frogs, jump to escape predators. Other animals, including antelope and goats, seem to jump because, well, it's fun.

But things that go up must come down. The sudden impact of landing puts enormous stress on bones, meaning that limb bones, particularly, must be able to handle many times their weight or risk breaking or shattering to pieces. For this reason, all animals built for jumping are also built for landing. Some animals, including kangaroos and humans, have found a way of recycling the force of impact, turning it into a springboard for the next leap.

LAUNCH IGNITION

Most small birds jump into the air as they begin to flap their wings. For this they require powerful muscles attached to their leg bones. In starlings, 90 percent of the energy involved in upward takeoff comes from the legs rather than the wings.

MOUNTAIN RANGING

Mountain goats are well known for being able to jump up and down steep cliff faces. Powerful muscles that attach to the scapulae provide the strength for jumping between boulders. They also have wide cloven hooves and dewclaws that work a little like ice picks.

Dewclaw

SHOWING OFF

Upon its long legs and toe bones, the male lesser florican springs into the air. After an elegant flap of its wing, it falls back into the grass while pulling a statue-like pose. This strange mating display is undertaken hundreds of times each day. The tallest and most statue-like jumpers attract the most females.

SIDEWAYS SIDLE

The sifaki uses its long legs to jump between branches, but sometimes it must move along the ground between trees. It jumps by leaping sideways, keeping its hands outstretched for balance.

Some jerboa species can manage a distance of almost 6½ feet/2 meters in a single bound.

LONG-EARED JERBOA
Euchoreutes naso

Deserts and parched grasslands offer little by way of food, but the long-eared jerboa has made such habitats its own by quite literally making every step count.

Jerboas spring themselves forward by catapulting their lightweight bodies off long, fused bones within their hind feet. Almost like tiny kangaroos, they range from place to place in search of insect prey, which they detect with large ears and keen eyes.

In such sparse habitats as the Gobi Desert, energy-saving adaptations are vital. The light weight of the jerboa skeleton is one such adaptation. Though their body is almost equivalent in size to a chicken's egg, long-eared jerboas weigh half as much. Rather than relying on muscle, which is a heavy tissue, the long-eared jerboa relies on special tendons for locomotion. These elastic tendons absorb the energy of each foot—landing, recycling, and reusing this energy for the next push-off. Essentially, each time it lands, the long-eared jerboa is propelled into the next step.

The long-eared jerboa depends on insects and spiders for food, and much of their skull anatomy is given over to the ears. Their skulls possess enlarged middle-ear cavities, which help them listen for the telltale sounds of prey in the cold desert night. In fact, they have the largest ear-to-body ratio of any animal on Earth.

Much like the cheetah, the long-eared jerboa uses its long tail as a counterbalance while running.

The long-eared jerboa has a tail almost twice as long as its body. A little like a car with four-wheel steering, jerboas use their long tail as an energy-saving counterbalance, allowing them to change direction quickly while traveling at high speed. This allows them to dodge the advances of predators, including their mortal enemy, the little owl.

In addition to enlarged middle-ear cavities, jerboas have large orbits that help them to spot both prey and predator.

RED KANGAROO
Macropus rufus

Kangaroos are supercharged athletes that manage something few animals can match—they possess both speed and endurance. The secret to their success comes from a skeleton brimming with adaptations that reduce weight and reuse elastic energy. Forget marathon running—kangaroos are marathon jumpers.

In a single leap, the red kangaroo can cover a distance of 26–29 feet/8–9 meters, reaching heights of almost 10 feet/3 meters.

They achieve this incredible feat by reusing the kinetic energy gathered from their previous jump. With each bounce, stout tendons in the kangaroo's legs turn kinetic energy into stored elastic energy that can be reused in the next leap. These tendons, attached to long bones on the legs, essentially catapult the body forward. This impressive adaptation means that kangaroos use far less energy when traveling at speed than other animals. In fact, what galloping horses manage in eight footsteps, kangaroos manage with two.

Kangaroos, like all marsupials, have a distinctive pair of epipubic bones that face forward out from the pelvis.

As with other leapers, including frogs and jerboas, kangaroos spring off long toes. In fact, most of their weight is taken on the lengthened fourth toe. The second and third toes are fused and provide a neat little comb for grooming their fur.

Kangaroos have impressively muscled tails. The long, bony tail of the red kangaroo serves partly as a counterbalance while running, but it can also be used as a handy prop when resting. But there's more to their tail than just this. Scientists recently discovered that kangaroos can use their tail like a third leg that pushes them forward when moving from low speed to high speed.

In fact, the force the tail exerts on the ground at low speeds generates more lift than the legs. The up-and-down motion of the tail while running helps to inflate the lungs, saving the kangaroo more energy. Male red kangaroos have even been known to use their tail as a sort of third leg from which to launch kicks at rival kangaroos.

Kangaroos have well-developed forearms that they use for boxing, for grasping food, and (in females) to open their pouch to check on joeys.

AMERICAN BULLFROG
Lithobates catesbeianus

The key characteristic of most frogs and toads is their long, powerful back legs, which can be adapted for a variety of purposes, including jumping, digging, and swimming. In the American bullfrog, these legs make for an explosive leap. The American bullfrog can jump ten times its body length, making it one of the most impressive leapers of its kind.

To find out how frogs manage this feat, scientists use slow-motion photography to study the muscles and bones in their legs. Like grasshoppers and locusts, frogs tense special tendons attached to their long legs just before they leap. As the body moves forward, they allow these tendons to snap back into place like elastic bands, catapulting the frog forward with a nitro-like injection of extra speed. The bones in their feet (tarsals, metatarsals, and phalanges) provide the foundation for added liftoff. Yet there is more to frogs than just their legs.

In most species, the bones of frogs are light and dramatically reduced. This allows them to stay in the air for longer.

Frogs barely have ribs—the short rib-like bones are actually a part of their spine, and frogs don't use them to breathe. Instead, they pull air in and out of their bodies by pumping their chins.

To allow for a safe landing, the American bullfrog has extra-strong limb bones. Unlike most vertebrates, the radius and ulna in the lower forearms are fused, as are the tibia and fibula in the lower legs. Frogs also benefit from a sternum, or breastbone, that works a little like a shock absorber.

The American bullfrog is, like all frogs, a creature shaped by predators. Every living frog you have ever seen is like a loaded spring, watchful for advancing carnivores. In the long legs held beneath their bodies, tendons are primed and readied for release. They jump. They land. They live another day.

The orbits of frogs are enormous, holding eyes that allow for 360-degree vision.

The first fossils of frogs—amphibians with distinctive long leg bones, a three-pronged pelvis, and a highly reduced tail—come from the Jurassic period, dating back to approximately 180 million years ago.

GLIDING AND FLIGHT

The only dinosaurs that remain today are those that took to the skies, the creatures we call birds. Today, almost 10,000 bird species rule the skies (and occasionally the land), and each has the same basic dinosaur pattern: two legs for walking and two forearms upon which arm and finger bones have been adapted into flapping sails that we call wings.

But birds are not alone in being airborne. Many bony animals have also taken to the skies and had their bones adapted into wings of different shapes and styles. Some, such as bats, are true fliers—like birds, their wings allow for powered flight with purpose. Others, such as flying squirrels or draco lizards, are gliders. Like paper airplanes, they can dive with style between trees or cliffs using flaps of skin or even long, webbed toes.

In vertebrates, the story of flight is really a story of bones stretching out generation by generation over many millions of years to become powered or gliding wings. And each animal family has its own unique skeletal adaptations that provide a life in the atmosphere above.

BIRDS

Bird skeletons are based on the two-legged dinosaurs (theropods) from which they evolved. The radius and ulna in the lower arm are long, and the wing ends in the alula—an adapted dinosaur "thumb." This thumb bone controls special flight feathers that, when stretched out, can assist in flying slowly or landing.

BATS

Within the wings of bats are four familiar mammal finger bones stretched wide over many millions of years. Their paired thumbs are clawed and stick out from the front of the wing to assist in gripping when not in flight. Like birds, they have incredibly light bones, which help to keep them airborne longer.

THE GLIDERS

A host of tree-living animals have evolved to become gliders that can move from tree to tree to find food or escape predators.

MICRORAPTORS

Unlike birds, some dinosaurs evolved four wings rather than two. *Microraptor* is one of a number of recently discovered fossils from China that show extra flight feathers attached to the legs. These extra wings may have helped *Microraptor* and its relatives maneuver through dense forests or allowed these reptiles to "parachute" onto their prey.

Slithering sails

While falling from the tops of trees, the so-called flying snake can suck in its abdomen and stretch its ribs wide to create a pseudo-concave wing. By continuing its s-shaped movement while falling, it can effectively slither through the air, landing up to 330 feet/100 meters away.

Skin flaps

About fifty species of flying squirrel exist. They have a long membrane called the patagium that stretches from wrist to ankle and allows them to glide almost 330 feet/100 meters to safety.

PTEROSAURS

This enormous family of flying reptiles dominated the skies for more than 150 million years. They flew with wings that were mostly held together by a dramatically lengthened fourth finger. From this finger was stretched a membrane made of muscle and skin that was capable of connecting with the hind legs to form a vast, flapping supersail.

BARN OWL
Tyto alba

To a rodent, a single look from a barn owl spells almost certain death. Its orbits are enormous, and they face directly forward, meaning that the field of vision in each eyeball overlaps. This provides binocular eyesight used to spot prey from above.

But big eyes come with problems in nature. Big eyes require internal structures to stop them from falling in on themselves. In birds, these internal structures come in the form of sclerotic rings. These bony rings limit the barn owl's ability to move its eyes around in its sockets as we can. Without eyes that can move independently of the skull, owls must move their entire heads to focus in on prey, and for that they need a neck like no other.

Like many owls, the barn owl has a neck that allows for 270-degree rotation. They manage this because they possess fourteen neck vertebrae, twice that of mammals. These neck vertebrae are largely saddle-shaped, allowing them a greater surface upon which to slide together and limiting the chance of damage during severe neck movements.

The beak is robust and hooked, which allows the barn owl to tear prey apart.

A special arrangement of veins and tissue means that the barn owl's blood flow is not interrupted even when its neck is twisted.

The fastest recorded flight
speed of the barn owl
is 50 miles/80 kilometers
per hour.

This unusual neck arrangement allows barn owls to scan the ground in nearly all directions as they fly on silent wings. But their sensory apparatus is about more than just sight. By swiveling their heads as they fly, they can also pick up telltale noises of scurrying prey using a pair of asymmetrical ear holes in the skull.

All birds of prey have strong wings that allow them to lift up prey and fly it back to the nest. Carrying this added weight burden requires long wing bones, which provide a broader surface area for extra lift. The bones in the foot, which are fused tarsal and metatarsal bones, are short and stout and provide the mechanism for working sharp claws capable of both carrying and killing.

The barn owl flies silently because of tiny serrations on the leading edge of the flight feathers, which reduce noise by breaking up the flow of the air over the wings.

COMMON FLYING DRAGON
Draco volans

In the treetops of Southeast Asia there exists a lizard with a secret. When being hunted by predators, this lizard relies on a truly spectacular adaptation. The common flying dragon can leap from trees and, as if by magic, unfurl vast wings upon which it glides away. But these are not wings like those of birds or bats. Their wings are an extension of their ribs.

Dragon lizards have a set of specially adapted ribs covered in a membrane of skin between the forelimbs and hind limbs. At rest, four or five of these thoracic ribs fold against one another and are held tight against the body. When spooked, dragon lizards erect these special ribs, creating giant sails via membranes called patagia, which catch the wind and can be used to escape.

But dragon lizards have another trick up their sleeve. Their wrist bones are more mobile than those of most lizards, allowing them to actually grasp their strange wing membranes as they fly. Using their claws, they can stretch their wing membranes extra wide after takeoff, much like a superhero using a cape to glide off a building.

The common flying dragon is assisted in its gliding flight by a long tail, which can be used like the rudder on an airplane to steer through the air. Their bones are light, allowing them to stay airborne longer. Some dragon lizards can make flights of 32 feet/ 10 meters or more from tree to tree, which is impressive for an animal little more than the size of a mouse.

But gliding flight isn't all about escaping predators. The common flying dragon is incredibly territorial. If a male spots an interloper on its turf, it will immediately swoop down, exposing its blue underside as a warning. Special yellow flaps behind its neck serve as an extra method of intimidation. Of course, these special flaps, called throat lappets, also help it glide.

The common flying dragon also uses its patagia to swoop down upon potential rivals.

While all other lizards breathe by expanding and contracting their rib cage, the flying dragon has adapted to use the muscles in its chest—its ribs are being used for something else!

The female common flying dragon has a pointy skull that she uses to dig burrows to lay her eggs in.

The bat has incredible control over its wings and can change direction with the slightest movement.

Wing muscles attach to the body via the large keel bone on the sternum.

LARGE FLYING FOX
Pteropus vampyrus

With a wingspan of up to 5 feet/1.5 meters, the large flying fox is the largest bat on Earth. Like us, this fruit bat has molar teeth, incisor teeth, and canine teeth; it has seven neck bones, a rib cage, and a pelvis, and, like us, it has distinctive mammal hands with four fingers and a thumb—a familiar mammalian skeleton, but this one is built for flight.

Unlike insects and birds, which have quite rigid wings that can only move in a few directions, bats have more than two dozen joints in their wings. They have a huge amount of control over how each joint moves, allowing them to adjust their flight accordingly.

A bat's patagium, or wing membrane, is supported by the arm and by four highly elongated fingers. The patagium extends all the way around to the bat's hind legs and tail, where it forms a flap called the uropatagium, supported by specialized foot bones called calcars. The uropatagium not only helps the bat fly and maneuver; in some bat species, it is also used to sweep prey, such as insects, into the bat's mouth while the bat is in flight.

The skull of the large flying fox is heavier than that of most bats. In some ways, its skull resembles a crash helmet. In large groups, the large flying fox will smash into the tree canopy, grabbing onto passing branches with its claws before tearing fruits apart with large canines and molars that are sharpened like scissor blades. Bats can break bones while landing in this way, but they are impressive healers.

Flying foxes are the largest members of the fruit bat family, the Megachiroptera. Most scientists think that by losing their ability to echolocate many millions of years ago, this large family of bats unlocked the ability to evolve to greater size. Today, there are 186 known species of living fruit bat, and the large flying fox is the biggest of them all.

Many fruit bats, including flying foxes, also drink from flowers. They lap up nectar with their long, hairy tongue which they keep rolled up deep within their rib cage when not being used.

RUNNING

In grasslands where predators lurk, it is often the fastest individuals that survive. In this way, over many years, the presence of predators causes prey to evolve. The skeletons of many prey species have therefore become adapted for speed.

But predators can also evolve. As prey get faster, so too must the predators. In this way, predator and prey can sometimes become entangled in an evolutionary battle that can go on for millions of years and reach dizzying speeds.

Running speed isn't only about short-distance races between predators and prey. Running fast can help animals in a number of ways, as you can see on these pages.

A.

B.

A. In their seasonal search for food, caribou make a journey of more than 3,000 miles/4,800 kilometers each year, occasionally clocking speeds of up to 50 miles/80 kilometers per hour. For them, time is of the essence. Their long leg bones and sturdy toe bones provide marathon-runner endurance. Like their predators, caribou are also built for sudden bouts of speed. Within twenty-four hours of being born, a caribou could outrun an Olympic sprinter.

B. African wild dogs work in packs to wear out and exhaust their fleeing prey. With comparatively sturdier legs than other dog species, they will hound and harass a potential meal for up to sixty minutes or more, maintaining speeds of up to 30 miles/48 kilometers per hour. Eventually their prey collapses with exhaustion and the kill is made.

C. Some crocodiles, such as Australian freshwater crocodiles, can gallop toward threats in an attempt to scare them off. By pushing off with both hind limbs at the same time, and landing with the forelimbs before pushing off again, their unusual running style resembles that of a rabbit. By galloping like this, they can manage a speed of 10 miles/16 kilometers per hour—pretty impressive for a crocodile on land.

D. Basilisk lizards have a running style like no other. When confronted by predators, they run on their hind legs toward water and sprint along the surface. Their long, bony claws are attached to flaps of skin that capture a layer of air bubbles, keeping the lizard afloat while it sprints. Young basilisks can run up to 65 feet/20 meters along the water's surface.

Special tendons in the feet, including the Achilles tendon, convert and recycle energy with enhanced efficiency while running.

HOMO SPRINTIAN

Compared to other primates, humans have a variety of skeletal features that help us to run long distances. For our overall size, the bones that make up human legs are long, so they propel the body forward using less energy per stride. Human leg bones also have large joint surfaces that more widely spread the forces created during running.

C.

D.

CHEETAH
Acinonyx jubatus

Occasionally reaching speeds of 70 miles/112 kilometers per hour, the cheetah is the fastest land animal on Earth. Each of its bones is optimized for speed, and its skeleton is chiseled to almost defy gravity.

The two most effective bony adaptations that the cheetah possesses are long legs and a long, flexible spine. Each time a cheetah's feet hit the ground, it flexes its spine, stretching its body out to maximize the distance between each stride. Stride length is also increased through lengthened lower leg bones, which push the body forward over greater distance.

With each thrust of the legs, the cheetah achieves a stride length that averages 22 feet/7 meters. For half of the time that it is sprinting, it has all four feet off the ground. Lightweight bones allow the cheetah to stay in the air longer, but come with a downside—they can break more easily. To reduce wear and tear on the lower leg bones, their tibia and fibula are bound tight, meaning that they work like shock absorbers.

The long, flexible tail acts as a counterbalance as the cheetah runs.

The pads of the cheetah's toes are patterned, like the soles of running shoes, and provide extra grip.

The cheetah's long tail can act as a counterbalance, allowing it to make sudden changes in direction while running at top speed. It also has long claws that grip like an athlete's cleats—the cheetah is a master of momentum.

As well as being the fastest land animal, the cheetah is the fastest at accelerating. The cheetah can achieve a speed of almost 50 miles/ 80 kilometers per hour in just two seconds, accelerating at roughly the speed of a rock falling from a cliff. Recent research involving the use of satellite trackers on wild cheetahs suggest that it is acceleration, rather than speed, that is the most critical part of a successful hunt.

The widened nasal passages allow for greater volumes of oxygen in and out of the lungs.

The cheetah's spine allows it to keep its head up and steady, so its eyes never leave its target as it sprints toward prey.

Speed is determined by both the length and the frequency of the stride, and the cheetah has perfected both of these things.

Ostriches have a stride length of up to 16 feet/5 meters.

Ostriches are well-adapted to spot predators. They possess long necks (with seventeen vertebrae) that help in scanning the horizon, and the largest of all land-living vertebrate eyes, measuring 2 inches/ 5 centimeters in diameter.

OSTRICH
Struthio camelus

Though the cheetah is celebrated as the fastest animal on land, the ostrich is the fastest over distance, and then some. Ostriches regularly reach speeds of 43 miles/70 kilometers per hour or more as they move across their grassland and desert habitats. They are the fastest sprinting birds on the planet.

For their size, the ostrich has the longest legs of any living flightless bird, achieving a stride length of up to 16 feet/5 meters. As with the cheetah, the ostrich's muscles are tightly packed high up into the body upon the femur bones in the thigh. This maximizes the power and rate at which the lower legs can be flicked forward and backward while running.

Ostriches use their feet to kick at their prey.

As with horses' hooves, ostrich feet are a slimmed-down and simplified version of what they once were. Where most birds walk on four toes, the ostrich is the only living bird to walk on two toes.

The big toe supports the majority of body mass, and the smaller toe acts like a stabilizer, helping the ostrich dodge advancing predators. Like a sprinter in running spikes, the larger claw can penetrate the ground while achieving high speeds, assisting with grip.

Yet even with these adaptations, the stamina and speed that ostriches so effortlessly maintain appear otherworldly. How do they manage it? The secret lies in their tendons, which are far more elastic than those of other creatures of their size. As they release

their elastic energy, these tendons fling the limb bones forward, providing 83 percent more output with each stride when compared to human sprinters.

So full of speed and stamina are ostriches that, if they were undertaking a 26-mile/42-kilometer marathon alongside the best human athletes, they would complete the race twice as fast, using half the energy that a human would require.

Pronghorns have been known to cover 7 miles/ 11 kilometers in just ten minutes.

PRONGHORN ANTELOPE
Antilocapra americana

Occasionally clocking speeds of 55 miles/ 88 kilometers per hour or more, the pronghorn antelope is the fastest land animal in the Americas. Yet what makes the pronghorn stand out from other sprinting animals is that it can endure speeds like this over very long distances. Pronghorn can maintain their top speed for around half a mile (almost a kilometer), more than enough to outrun its predators.

The secret of the pronghorn's success lies mostly in its leg bones. As with its giraffe and okapi cousins, the pronghorn antelope takes much of its weight on two long pointed toes that are specially cushioned to limit the impact of each step. Its long toe bones increase stride length so that each push off the ground gathers greater distance. The pronghorn antelope also possesses special interlocking grooves in the joints of its leg bones, which ensure that they move together almost as if on hinges. This limits the likelihood

of sprains and fractures. The ulna and radius are partially fused, a trait that further limits the likelihood of breakage.

The pronghorn antelope has a large, barrel-shaped rib cage in which is found an impressive windpipe, giant lungs, and a slightly larger than expected heart, which helps pump blood to the muscles of the legs. As with many prey species, the orbits of pronghorn antelope are large and point sideways, meaning that pronghorns can keep an almost 360-degree watch for predators.

Predators have clearly had a big impact on the pronghorn antelope. Their speed hints that, at one point in recent history, they lived alongside a very fast predator that must have provided the driving force for their evolution. The prime candidate is the mysterious American cheetah, a creature that disappeared from the North American plains more than 10,000 years ago.

As with giraffes, skin covers a bony skull outcrop that makes up the horns. In pronghorns, a hardened sheath that covers them is shed and regrown each year.

The pronghorn's scapula, in the shoulder, lies flat against the side of the chest, where its rotation swings the powerful forelimbs forward and backward.

Though not a true antelope, it is known as such because of its resemblance to the antelopes of Africa and Asia.

SWIMMING

Moving through water is more difficult than moving through air because water molecules bind tightly with one another. This means that underwater creatures often have streamlined skeletons that slice through water, giving them a fusiform (torpedo-like) shape.

Moving through water also requires a means to propel the body forward. While many animals, such as whales and sailfish, depend on muscle-laden tail vertebrae to drive the body forward, some creatures have hit upon other skeletal adaptations to push their way through water, as you can see on these pages.

ROWING

Leatherback turtles have long bony flippers measuring up to 9 feet/2.7 meters, which they use to row the body forward. They use their hind legs to steer their body through the water. Leatherback turtles are the only living sea turtles that lack a bony upper shell, called a carapace.

FLAPPING

Manta rays propel themselves forward by undulating enormous flattened pectoral fins that can measure more than 22 feet/ 7 meters tip to tip. Unlike many rays, manta ray mouths point forward—this helps oxygenate their gills and sieve tiny particles of food from the water.

CRAWLING

The tub gurnard has long pectoral spines that project from the sides of the body. They use these spines like fingers to help them move across the bottom of the sea. These strange spines are also highly sensitive to movement. They help the gurnard detect potential prey beneath the sand.

UNDULATING

Pipefish have an armor-plated skeleton with a long dorsal fin that is capable of undulating like a ribbon. These frequent undulations move in waves down the body, powering forward movement. This helps the pipefish move quietly through its seagrass habitats without drawing attention from predators.

CONVERGENT EVOLUTION

Throughout the history of life on Earth, fusiform shapes have ruled the oceans. Here are two very different skeletons that have happened upon the same streamlined body shape.

Ichthyosaurs were fish-like reptiles that ruled the oceans during the middle of the age of dinosaurs. Like whales and dolphins, these reptiles evolved from land-living creatures. Inside their two pairs of fins are the remnants of limb bones.

Dolphins have long pectoral fins that contain the finger bones of their land-living ancestors. Their muscular tail is attached to a spine that goes up and down. Their tail is flattened horizontally rather than vertically.

BLACK MARLIN
Istiompax indica

The black marlin is one of the world's fastest fish, sometimes reaching speeds of more than 80 miles/129 kilometers per hour as it travels through the open ocean. Its missile-shaped skeleton has been fine-tuned to travel fast in short bursts, all the while using the least amount of energy possible.

To propel itself through water, the black marlin uses its strong, muscular tail. Along its spine are numerous places where muscles attach. Many of these muscles are "high-twitch" muscles that allow for intense bursts of power.

Unlike other marlins, the black marlin has pectoral fins that are locked in place. Like enormous airplane wings, they maintain upward lift and stabilize the marlin as it glides through its watery environment. A long, thick dorsal fin, which looks almost like a crest, offers added support.

Marlin skeletons may grow more than any other creature on Earth. When baby marlin first hatch from eggs, they are about the size of a pea. As adults, less than ten years later, they reach more than 14 feet/4 meters in length and may be as much as a million times heavier.

Marlin are best known for their pointed upper jaw, the rostrum. With this sword-like adaptation, the black marlin is like a knife that cuts through the water.

But there is more to its sword than this. Marlin can swipe their rostrum at passing shoals of fish like a master fencer, stunning and killing those fish that accidently get too close. Recent scientific research has shown that it is reinforced along its top and sides, making it much stronger than it looks. Though almost iron-like, marlin bills do occasionally snap off. Sometimes they are found impaled in other sea creatures, including sharks.

Unlike most fish, the marlin has a rostrum, or beak, that is capable of healing if it is scratched or dented.

The black marlin uses its powerful tail to move through the water, reaching speeds of 80 miles/129 kilometers per hour.

BLUE WHALE
Balaenoptera musculus

With a skeleton that can support 220 tons/200 metric tons of flesh, the blue whale is perhaps the biggest animal that has ever lived. Almost every single bone has been stretched to the limits of physics.

The blue whale is an ocean traveler that can sometimes cover almost 280 miles/450 kilometers in a single day as it journeys between feeding places. Like a giant ocean liner, it is powered by an impressive engine—a tail densely packed with muscles that account for 40 percent of its weight.

These muscles attach to the lower spine of the blue whale. Each tail vertebra is more than 3 feet/1 meter wide and contains outstretched regions called neural spines and transverse processes, the bony projections on either side of the vertebrae onto which broad tail muscles can attach. Unlike in most mammals, the middle part of the spine is rigid, rather like an iron girder.

Blue whales grow to such enormous size partly because of their bounteous food source, krill. Using vast bony plates made of fingernail-like material called baleen that hang from their long jaws,

The last few caudal vertebrae are flattened out to support the heavy, powerful tail flukes.

Unlike toothed whales (which have five sets of finger bones), many baleen whales have four fingers within their flippers.

they sieve these tiny crustaceans from the water with the help of a powerful tongue. The whale's top jaw is fused to the skull and provides the anchoring required for these heavy baleen plates.

Though well adapted to the ocean, blue whale skeletons retain many of the features of their land-living mammalian ancestors. They have four sets of phalanges in each flipper, two shoulder blades called scapulae, seven stiff neck vertebrae, and a distinct nostril that forms the blowhole. Indeed, their spine moves up and down like a mammal rather than left and right like a fish. There are even vestigial bones found deep within the belly that hint at their land-living past. These unusual bones are the remains of tiny hind limbs that today serve no purpose, rather like the tailbone of apes and the wings of the flightless kiwi.

A blue whale skull is around 20 feet/6 meters long, but due to the dimensions of its throat, it cannot swallow anything larger than a beach ball.

EMPEROR PENGUIN
Aptenodytes forsteri

On land, emperor penguins look almost comical. But under the water, a penguin is a fish-eating submarine torpedo, with a skeleton chiseled to perfection for flying through aquatic environments.

Compared to flying birds, penguins have very heavy bones. They lack the air pockets that most birds possess, which reduces their buoyancy (the ability to float in water) and allows them to chase fish far deeper than expected without being pulled back up. Emperor penguins have been known to dive as deep as 1,640 feet/500 meters below the water, a feat impossible without weighty bones.

Flying through water is harder than flying through air. The density of water means that every flap takes more energy. Every thrust takes effort. But penguins make use of something that aerial birds cannot—the upward stroke.

Most flying birds make use of downward strokes only to gather lift, but penguins—being surrounded on all sides by liquid—can generate thrust from both upward and downward strokes. For this reason, compared to birds that fly, they have highly developed muscles associated with upward flapping that attach to giant paddle-like shoulder blades (scapulae).

And then there are the phalanges, the bones within the fingers. Within their wings, most birds possess three fingers onto which are anchored feathers, particularly those feathers that guide steered flight and controlled landings. Penguins, of course, have little need for such feathers.

Their phalanges instead have become long and flat, almost like a pancake. The third finger, normally tiny in birds, is enormous in penguins. These wide phalanges improve the surface area of the wing, greatly influencing the thrust that they can achieve with

The beak of the penguin is long and thin and lined with throat teeth—hard, backward-pointing projections inside the mouth that mean that once caught, a fish cannot escape.

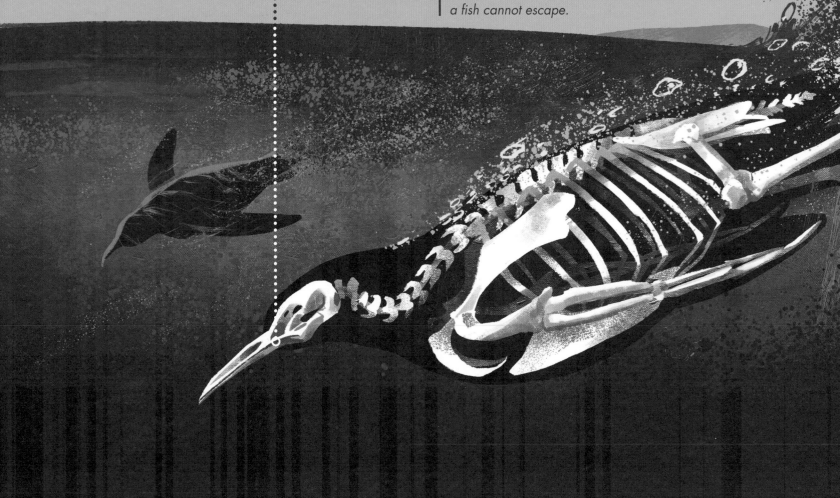

each wing stroke. These are the engines that propel penguins forward during the chase, after all.

Their stomachs full, they come back to land. Shuffling, squawking, ungainly once again. And we chuckle, unaware of the aquanautic feats that such a skeleton permits beneath the waves.

The penguin skeleton tapers at the top and the bottom, a classic fusiform shape, rather like a dolphin or a swordfish. This reduces drag while swimming and allows them to cut through the water easily.

All penguins have unusually fused tail vertebrae that form a structure called the pygostyle. While on land, some species use it as a third leg, a sort of prop to rest on—almost like a bike with its kickstand down.

GLOSSARY

baleen: the bony plates found in the mouths of some whales, used to filter food

carapace: a hard shell sometimes made of bone or chitin

carnassials: molars or pre-molar teeth adapted for shearing flesh rather than tearing it

carnivore: an animal that eats meat

cartilage: a flexible type of connective tissue. Some animals have skeletons made only of cartilage.

chondrocytes: special cells found in cartilage that allow it to be more elastic

coccyx: a set of bones at the bottom of the spine that represent a vestigial tail

diastema: a gap between teeth

dorsal: related to the back

echolocation: a technique used by some animals, like whales and bats, to locate objects using reflected sound, or echoes

evolution: the gradual changes observed in a species over time, caused primarily by natural selection

femur: thigh bone

fibula: one of two bones in the lower hind limb

foramen magnum: the hole in the base of the skull where the spinal cord enters

fusiform: a shape that narrows at both ends

herbivore: an animal that eats plants

hyoid bone: a bone in the front of the neck

incisors: front teeth adapted for cutting

keel: a curved extension of the breastbone onto which flight muscles attach in birds and bats

keratin: a protein that makes up hair, fingernails, feathers, hooves, and horns

kinetic energy: energy generated by movement

ligament: connective tissue that links bones

mandible: jaw bone

marrow: a soft, fatty substance found in the center of bones

metatarsals: long bones of the foot between the tarsals and the phalanges

omnivore: an animal that eats both meat and plants

orbits: eye sockets

osteoderms: hard bony structures on the skin, such as scales and plates

patagium: a membrane that connects the fore and hind limbs of an animal, allowing it to fly or glide

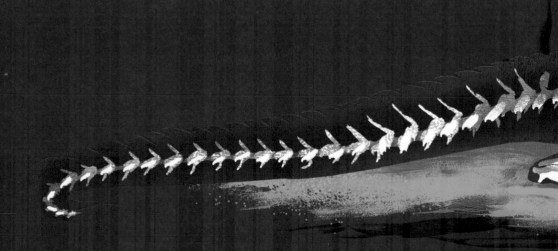

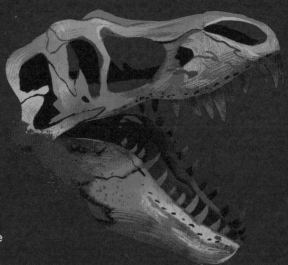

pectoral: related to the chest

prehensile: capable of grasping, like a tail or a trunk

processes: special ridges

pygostyle: a fused tailbone that occurs in some birds

radius: one of the two bones in the forelimbs

rostrum: a beak-like projection evolved from the jawbone, as in a marlin

sagittal crest: a ridge of bone that runs along the top of the skull from the back to the front

scapula: shoulder blade

sclerotic rings: rings of bone in the eye

sesamoid: wrist bone

sternum: breastbone

tarsals: bones of the hind foot and midfoot

tibia: one of two bones in the lower hind limb

ulna: one of the two bones in the forelimbs

vertebrae: bones that make up the spinal column

vertebrate: an animal with a backbone

vestigial structure: a part of the body that remains despite the fact that it no longer serves a purpose, such as the pelvis in a snake or the tailbone in a person

zygomatic arch: cheekbone

ABOUT THE AUTHOR

Jules Howard is a zoologist, nonfiction author, and international ambassador for science. As well as writing regularly for the *Guardian* and the BBC, he offers support to a number of nonfiction book publishers working on zoological themes.

ABOUT THE ILLUSTRATOR

Chervelle Fryer is an illustrator hailing from Cardiff, Wales. She specializes in character illustration and loves to work with organic themes in bright colors and heavy textures.